god-shot

noun

a term used in recovery to reference something
profound or sometimes an intuitive thought that
provides motivation to continue in or start the
recovery process

Edited, designed, and founded by Rebecca Rijsdijk
@rebeccarijsdijk | rebeccarijsdijk.com

sundaymorningsattheriver.com
@sundaymorningsattheriver
hello@sundaymorningsattheriver.com
Thanks for reading.

God shots Wanted: Apply Within

poems by
Emily Perkovich

Contents

About the author

About the Publisher

Note on Previous Publications

Foreword/trigger warning

This book should be read with care. There are a multitude of triggers touched on, most notably, domestic and sexual abuse, suicidal ideation, self-harm, addiction, eating disorders, death and grief, and mental health disorders and diagnosis. Regarding these triggers, I feel that it is imperative to mention that this collection is a journey through trauma and to set expectations and reminders surrounding that.

A frequent concern that I have seen expressed in relation to art of this nature is the romanticism of unhealthy habits. I am not condoning unhealthy coping mechanisms, but they are real, and I believe they should be addressed rather than stigmatized. Many trauma victims experience a backlash to a point that they do not feel comfortable sharing and experience intense self-deprecation. This makes any journey to recovery or healing feel not only unattainable but also like a topic that they should not be talking about. I want my work to speak in a way that makes others feel comfortable sharing their experiences and comfortable feeling their emotions, whether positive or negative, without experiencing guilt for those emotions.

Childhood traumas in particular can be perceived differently for the child than they are for the adults surrounding them. That perception (whether real or exaggerated) can have a lasting impact on adult life. With that being said, while many childhood traumas are examined in this collection, I have a strong relationship with my parents now that I am an adult, and the perception of my experiences should not be used to judge the characters of the people surrounding me in this instance. People grow and change (myself included), and I believe forgiveness can play an important role in the changing of relationships and character. I am not writing an acknowledgment page, but I feel it is necessary to mention that I have a constantly growing support system, and I am eternally grateful to them for sticking with me through my lows and highs and how I express them. This is especially appreciated when negative feelings are surrounding the experiences.

Additionally, I am sensitive to the fact that not every person will be able to experience any sort of reconciliation with their traumas or the people involved, and I believe that should be regarded as equally acceptable.

Lastly, while I feel I have addressed most triggers, I leave a large amount of my work open for interpretation. I realize this means that this collection may trigger you in ways that I may not have thought of. I think it is important to not let your triggers hold you back from experiencing life, but please be gentle with yourself and self-aware when reading.

Emily, *June 2021*

Accident Forgiveness

Crash the car, crash the car, crash the car,
Don't fucking crash the car.
Crash the car,
Don't fucking crash the car.
But that's what I want.
You have kids at home.
Ok.
Fuck.
Crash the car,
Don't fucking crash the goddamn car.
Crash.
Shut the fuck up. We just fucking went over this.
Right.
Scream.
Ok scream but can you just...
Fuck,
Fuck,
Fuckkkkkk.
You need to stop.
The road is wet...
You're not crashing the car.
What if...
Don't fucking crash the car.
Pills.
Would you just fucking stop tonight??
No. Pills.
Go to sleep.
After pills.
What is your fucking problem?

You didn't let me crash the car...
Stop.
Stop,
Stop,
Stop.
Exhale,
Exhale,
Exhale, exhale, exhale, exhale,
What happens at empty?

Interview With The Eulogy

Where was the point of impact?

I was barefoot in the hallway, I can't remember if we had carpet
between rooms, the carpet In the living room was brown, and I
always thought that was lucky because sometimes if I didn't eat
dinner, the meal would end up buried in my face, but I clenched
my teeth, and the volcano in my nose would erupt onto the floor

No, stop making that joke with the broken finger that hurts
everywhere. The question is where did he hit you?

That depends on when you're asking, and I suppose when
depends on who, or maybe when is who, but I don't think who
has to be when, because there were definitely witnesses just not
to every when and there wasn't a who for every who

That's not what I mean. The first time he did something to hurt
you?

My mama hemorrhaged when I was born, and the way I've heard
it, he cut the cord and held me before she did, so they could
staunch the bleeding

I'm going to ignore that. Did he ever act out of violence?

At night, he'd throw back bottles, smoke, and his words came out
loud until my mama cried, and then my words would come out
loud, but I think the issue was in the water, or the issue was in
the bottles, or the issue was in my mama, and his hands had an

issue with my mama

We're trying to find the root. The onslaught. What caused the
affliction. What is your first painful memory?

Then you were asking about the hallway, what came next was the
gun, but before that, I held my sister, and after that there were
police

What do you remember? Did he live?

I can't say what I remember, only that there were no shots fired,
only that they confiscated the weapon, but they left behind his
hands, and I think it might have been more prudent to take the
hands, but what do I know except that guns don't kill people,
hands kill people, but I think he lived, even if I didn't

How did that make you feel?
How did that make you feel?
Answer the question.
How did that make you feel?
Hello?
How did that make you feel?

The number you have reached has been disconnected.

(I)d(I)o(m(e)s

I collect people like canker sores in the mouth of a masochist.
Raw-flesh kept wet. And the blush of it turns white with how it
can't grow back over new. I build them up along my gums. Let
them tear across the scarred, pink insides of my cheeks. Throat
craving slow-crawl of saliva, copper-tinged. How many ulcers
does it take to get to the center of my mouth? Wait. That's not
how that goes...but, then again, this narcissist wasn't built in a
day. And I only know how to write about me. It's like searching
for you in a me-stack...huh. Not sure about that one. I am
eating myself alive because nothing else knows how to fill me.
Ouroboros, self-devouring. I am diving into my own rib cage.
Grave-digging my innards. Viscera-cemetery. Mausoleum-me.
Maybe I can kill two relationships with one mental breakdown.
Throw enough bodies into graves. Eventually, something will
stick. Damn it. Wrong again. And nothing stays buried anyway.
Stop tonguing that ache. It'll never heal.

Pull String In Case Of Emergency

I'm a mass grave of a million parts, none of them mine. I am a strangled skeleton of angst and scars. And once I think I was mine. Then they scrawled their ink across my bones. Used as the well to pour their stories into. Used as the paperweight to hold down their pain. The halfway house that keeps them warmed and fed. I'm the undertaker, cleaning the mess out of their insides. I'm the wrists they cut when the darkness insisted it be bled. And I'm the leech that sucked out the emotions that were bursting from their straight jacket bodies. The veins where they stuck their needles, dirty and diseased, once the sharps box had been filled. And the carpet that soaked up the inside of all the broken bottles. I'm the gutter that helps the flood down off the roof just before it jumps. And the ladder they used to climb back to the top. They asked me to carry it all. And suddenly it was mine. Or maybe I was theirs. But once. I think I was mine.

I Still Don't Talk At Holiday Parties

In a dream, I invite my father over for dinner. In a dream, I speak with my hands. I press the index and middle finger on each hand together, then fling what they're holding away

they're holding nothing and I'm saying, I'm lost
In a dream, I flourish both hands out to my right and push myself away, and my father loads the word abandoned into the barrel of a gun

I hold up 3 fingers on each hand and the light blushes at my innocence

I am speaking with my hands, but I don't know most words, so in a dream, I clear the table by pressing my face down into the dirty plates. I pull the table cloth out from under the dishes, and it's actually a quilt, and the food crashes to the floor, and I suffocate on things I didn't want, and I leave my bed to stop the crying that started in the closet

The ceiling is yellowed, and the walls are suicidal, when I put two fingers to the temple and close my thumb down to shoot

I don't know how to speak with my hands, so in a dream, I stare into my father's eyes. I hope that when I cry, he swallows the tears and teaches me a new way to deal with the things that I locked up in the attic the attic is empty shadows

But even in the dream, he agrees with the word gun, and I hold
up an amber alert so that he knows that what I meant by the
milk carton was that this is where I learned how to fix things

I press a bullet into his palm and a pill into my own

I paint the scene in red, I swallow the scene in blue

Library Forensics

i) i never require company to take off their shoes. no surprise that i keep finding footprints. no one ever wiped their feet.

  a) open-door policies lead to unwanted guests, and i've had a hard time keeping track of who's been renting and who is here for good.

  b) open-book policies make it difficult to ascertain who read the facts and who just wrote in the margins.

    1) some damage is evident. a coffee ring here, ripped edges there. i find more dog-eared pages these days than i'd like to, but i just keep unfolding corners. not that the wrinkles disappear. but they're easier to look past.

ii) long-forgotten tenant leaves a microscope.

  a) there are more fingerprints than i once realized.

    1) i know who these fingerprints belong to.

    2) i don't know who all of these fingerprints belong to.

  b) tear stains smudge the ink.

    1) salt crystals cluster.

  c) tear stains are harder to look at than fingerprints.

iii) it would have been smarter to use a timestamp. it would have been smarter to alphabetize. no. to place in chronological order. no. these pages are all tearing. these pages are all mixing. how many books do i have here?

iv) i hire a cleaning service.

   a) the footprints have stuck in wet cement. i didn't realize they were here when the foundation was poured.

      1) i should have hired an exorcist.

      2) i should have sold the property.

      3) i should have burned this place down.

v) i should have burned this place down.

16

remember the sunday-night strobe lights/remember flooding
that basement with resentment and regret/i punched you, and
you threw me into a wall and then threw the guy next to me
for good measure/he hit the left edge of me, and there was a
body-sized hole in the drywall, but no one seemed to care/i saw
it in flashes while they hit the lights over and again, but the floor
was slick, and by the time we got up off the ground it seemed
inconsequential/i sweat off my make-up, and we passed out beer-
soaked in the bedroom on the first floor/i woke up bruised and
smiling/and sometimes i still wake up bruised, smiling

but we don't hold hands anymore
we don't make eye contact anymore

because of that other time/remember that time/it was when i
took advantage of your aching, and you took advantage of my
loneliness/i read to you while you watched tv/and there was
no strobe light, but the blue had a bit of a flicker/i passed out
in my clothes, and you were still beer-soaked and flooded with
resentment, and i was still sweating out all my regrets/and you
played itsy-bitsy-spider up my left thigh/and your hand left a
body-shaped hole in my chest/no one really seemed to notice/
and when i woke up a weekend later, and it was already easter
sunday, it seemed inconsequential/and i don't sleep smiling
anymore/but sometimes i still wake up bruised

In The Dirt

My shorts are wet. I pissed myself. I'm too old for this. I know
I'm too old for this. But I can't go inside. Inside is where the
leaving happens. Leaving is where the yelling happens. Yelling
is...
Stop.
The sandbox is staining the white denim. I won't be able to hide
it. But I can't go inside.
Stop.
The air is flooded with spring. Catalpa trees and fresh earth.
Cherry and apple blossoms. This is my safe place. I'm pumping
my legs to keep the swing going, and I have to pee, but if I keep
moving, maybe, I'll forget, I'll be distracted, I'll be able to hold
it, I'll fly away, take to the sky, they'll be distracted, I'll fly away,
I'll fly away, I'll fly away, they'll be distracted, I'll fly away, they'll
never know, I'll fly away,
Stop.
I miss a beat.
Touch down on hard ground. The impact punches through me. I
clench my entire body. Brace against the fall. Hold back the tears.
My bladder releases.
Stop.
I'm building sandcastles amid the smell of piss.

Sacrosanct

I'm kneeling/sinking/drowning in sand. I always wondered
about the sand. And she's crying, again. She's barefoot/smoking/
crying. Head-in-hands praying. She's always head-in-hands, and
I'm left fingers-in-ears. I'm skeptic-eyes-rolling. I'm face- turned-
skyward, wishing someone would answer her. But I'm
never praying. I said wishing, not praying. I'm kneeling/sinking/
drowning in sand. And there are bowls full of mud. And bowls
full of rocks. And bowls filled with tears. And bowls brimming
with grass. And bowls teeming with berries. And there are bowls
filled with tears. And there are bowls bursting with stars. And
this bowl is empty. And I'm adding everything in pinches and
drops. And I'm fingers-in-ears. And she's mouthful-of-smoke,
praying. And maybe if I bless the tears. Call it makeshift-holy-
water. Call it baptism. Call it sacred. Call the berries wine.
Call the rocks body-of-christ. Call it anointed. Call the mud
resurrection. Call it divine. Call me god-fearing-converted.
Call me devout. Call it wishing/praying/pretending. Call me
kneeling/sinking/drowning. Call it baptism. Give me three days.
Make me a miracle. Make me believe. Make me the reason.
And I'm stirring. And I'm mixing. And I'm wishing. And she's
barefoot/smoking/crying. And I'm waiting. And there's never
any Passover. The firstborn always dies.

Dwell

I've been watching ghosts all night again
they tell me how I'm empty
they tell me I didn't take my pills yet
But I think that bottle was full yesterday?
they cry about how you'll never love me
how the bathtub is better flooded and face down
they cram their fingers down my throat to teach me what it's like
to be small
and they promise that I can fly if the ledge is high enough
/think about fire think about crashing think about drowning
think about starving think about pills and pills and think about
bullets and ropes and knives and think about ghosts/
and think, am I haunted?
Am I haunted?

This is Performance-Art

Wake without baby. Where is baby? Remember darkness.
Remember nurses. Remember doctors. Remember baby. Where
is baby?

Rewind to hospital bed. Rewind to phone in hand. Rewind to
head full of fire. Swallow pain. Swallow ache. Swallow his
voice. Reach for his voice. Realize he isn't coming. Realize your
mistake. Realize your options. Realize he isn't coming. Body
shakes. Jaw slacks. IV-line rip from the skin. Spasm. Seizure.
Mother screams. Doctor screams. Realize he isn't coming.
Realize it's dark. Realize he isn't coming. Realize your mistake.
Realize your options. Don't watch this. Don't watch this.

Fast-forward to bathtub. Fast-forward to fogged-mirror. Fast-
forward to empty-bottle and dizzy understanding that it won't be
enough. Swallow the way your body is giving up on the moment.
Swallow the baby crying in the room under the stairs. Swallow
spinning-heat. Realize your mistake. Realize your options. Reach
down throat. Teeth brush knuckles. Teeth brush wrist. Fingers
brush wet flesh. Wet-flesh reflex. Realize it's a dry heave. Realize
you're dehydrated. Realize your mistake. Realize your options.
Wake up. Wake up.

Slow-motion swallow from faucet. Slow-motion realize
conscious-slipping. Slow-motion brush his voice away. Hot
water, hit stomach lining. Room spin. Intestinal-simmer. Realize
your mistake. Realize your options. Retch out fire. Retch out
acid. Retch out devotion. Retch out yearning. Retch out husband.
Realize you're faint. Realize you're caving. Realize your mistake.

Realize your options. Let it out. Let it out.

Pause at the way the vomit floats on the surface. Pause at the baby crying. Pause at the way you need sleep. Brush away sleep. Brush away heat. Realize your mistake. Realize your options. Pause and swallow. Pause and release. Pause and realize this is it. Realize surrender. Realize you're staying. Realize your mistake. Realize your options. Don't sleep. Don't sleep.

How The Tooth-Fairy Ate The Candy-Man

You were smiling. I know you were smiling.

and we were young, I swear we were so young, we were young and in love, and we were young, when you laid us out in thin, white lines, and you snorted our youth in bumps and sold it in baggies and bargained with police, selling our years for a good time, we were young, and we only knew a good time, we were young, and it was love.

I swear it was young love.

But you kept saying open wide. Teeth hold secrets. And secrets keep you young. And we're young, and it's love. Open wide. Come on, lovely, just open wide. And I'm all hollow-smile through chipped teeth. And you yank. Baby teeth, baby. Baby teeth. Because secrets keep us young. Ground them into dust. Ground away our youth. Your skin all dressed in pain, just like I'm used to. And you crush me the way I always knew you would. Just like I'm used to.

but I swore it was love, it was young love, and you smiled, and it was sweet, and it was love, and I'm all cavities and love, because your smile has always made my teeth ache, and our years were always a good time, we were such a good time.

I swear it was a good time.

Tell Me What's Fun?

i.

Heat, press against you. Exit body, exit body. Emergency-exit
fucking room. Steamed breath, press sticky against windows.
Swallow his request. Swallow his pushing. Exit body. Ignore
his pushing. Ignore your softness. Ignore your heat. Ignore his
softness. Remember the ache. Remember the matched
heartbeats. Remember the hands pressed to hands. Remember
when you wanted this. Remember when he wanted you.
Remember it as wanting. Imagine it as wanting.

ii.

He took too much. But once he smelled like summer. Once he
was the beach. Once he was warm breath colliding against
warm breath. And he took too much. But once he was soft eyes.
Once he was whispered secrets against neck. And I'm sorry that
I always let him take too much. And I'm sorry I make him take
too much. But imagine it as wanting.

iii.

And I'm never enough. He's holding me-transparent, and
looking right through. But remember it as wanting. Remember it
as wanting. Imagine it as wanting.

Syncope

have i told you lately, about how i miss your hands around my
throat? all this inhale, exhale, repeat, repeat is exhausting.
　　just crush my windpipe next time
my lungs are rioting, again. on strike. better benefits, or we hold
our breath. don't test us, we'll do it.
　　i looked it up
you can't suffocate yourself. you can't suffocate yourself.
repetition equals emphasis
　　i looked it up
you can't suffocate the willing?
　　but i didn't look that up
what i mean is, you can't suffocate yourself. maybe if i keep
screaming, i'm not doing so well. it's like exhale, exhale,
　　breathe
　　emphasis here
　　out.
not in. out, not in. decrease blood-flow, decrease blood-flow,
faint. but, you can't suffocate yourself.
　　i looked it up
　　also known as, emphasis here
　　also known as, repetition
　　also known as
i miss your hands around my throat. i miss your hands
　　emphasis here

If One Of Them Is Dead

I planted a FOR SALE sign at the back of my throat. But what it
really advertises is how the corner of my mouth and my arteries
like to give away my secrets for free. It's like trying to have
an estate sale at a free clinic. It's like I'm selling an unwanted
teen pregnancy disguised as a love letter with no postage. Like
the word rape disguised as the condom failing. Hunger pangs
dressed up in "I just ate". An addict addicted to addicts claiming
they just enjoy the coffee at the meetings. My tongue is a trick
and a rat. Snitches get stitches. But fuck sewing her shut. Waste
of thread. I'll let her bleed out. Bite down to silence the screams.
Maybe next time I won't have to gag her.

Whir

I was born with buzzing in my head. At first, I thought bees. I am good at building honeycomb walls. Little, sticky bits of ache slip through. But most of the happy grows wings to flutter away. It's easier to leave than stay. I am not honeycomb-shaped. I am no shape at all. It can't be bees. My mouth has never dripped liquid sugar. More like oil spills. Still, underneath-tacky. Prism-meniscus, bouncing light across its own surface. Things that are pretty to look at, but toxic once swallowed. Spilled oil. Now that's a thought. Maybe I have a leak. Engine-ruptured. Hoses, tangled and bursting. Shadow-sludge, dripping off grey matter. Then again. Oil cleans. At some point, I would have been grace-filled. Well-kept. And I'm all sacrilege. Polluted. That doesn't work. Something else. Buzzing. Thrumming. Ceaseless. But also, phantom. Could be a hologram. That could fit. Substance-lacking. An idea. Haunting. All-electric shock, humming across my cognitive cage. High voltage. Explosion-poised. Ready. The only flaw there is the amount of power it would take to sustain that type of operation. I am energy-spent. More of a frayed extension cord than dynamic force. Strong enough to shock, but not enough for a constant surge. Like the broken fan-blade throwing everything off-kilter. Tick, tick, clank. A window-unit AC. Not a new model. But the ones from a few decades back. Constant-rattle of hot air pulsing against busted metal, cooling-coil. Antiquated, useless. I function at 1,000 BTU. Max capacity. It's so fucking depressing. Can't keep up. Never enough. And then I'm crying. So now there's the possibility of low-power electricity jumping against the rapid current of tears making a quick trek from my eyes to my collarbones. I'm getting off-track. Track. Trek. And then it hits me. The droning, purring, buzzing vibration never leaves. My depression owns a treadmill.

When Ana Was Born

You are raw egg hands. You are raw chicken hands. You are
bruised-brows, bitten-tongues, locked-doors, bathtub-hiding,
bloodied-knuckles hands. You are smoothing, tucking, tidying.
You are garden-sheared hands clipping yourself into a more
enviable skeleton. You are hair-curled, waist-slim, electric-
skinned in shadows and lace. You are hairspray and bleach and
ocean-eyeshadow over seaweed-irises. And that must be why I
was born drowning in your eyes. I am measuring myself against
the way I would fit too snug if you swallowed me whole. I am
all olive and curves. I roll across myself in hills instead of waves,
while you flow into hipbone tributaries and ribcage-levies. But
erosion is inherited, so when my stomach growls, I remember
how I was born from a siren, all dressed in divinity, and I let my
canyon-echoes ring. They sing themselves into fetal-void. Me, all
pregnant with starvation. And your knobby knees knelt in
the dirt of me, planting the seeds, but the moment of conception
came from violence. It was my face pressed deep into a dinner-
plate mess. And I keep trying to piece together the labor
and delivery. I keep looking for the moment the aversion to
sustenance crowned. Was it the way your cheekbones cradled
your thin smile? The way your ethereal hands shushed and
hushed post-destruction? I can't be sure. But I remember the
way my hair hung limp, brushing my too-buried collar bones,
greased with fried-chicken skin. My nose bled out mashed
potatoes and gravy as after-birth. And you handed me silence, so
I named her famine.

Jane Doe Plays Russian-Roulette And Wins

I'm unzipping body bags, like unpacking suitcases.

Here are the victims, and they are all me. Don't ask where I've hidden the souvenirs. Those are me too, and they just dredge up the past. Claw open old wounds.

I'm unzipping body bags, and I don't know where to put what is spilling out.

My hands are tied. My hands are full. My hands are...those aren't my hands. I never authorized an exhumation. There's blood on my hands. I don't want to revisit these graves.

I'm unzipping body-bags, but I already buried my dead.

I know this from every angle. It catches light there, hides it here. I am these shadows.

I'm unzipping body bags, and they are cocked and loaded.

I know the way the bullet sounds in the space between late night and early morning. How it echoes back. Remember, you did this? I know the way the bullet feels as it ties itself tight around my neck. Rough and knotted. Lover's kiss, caressing my collar bones. I know the way the bullet tastes as it slides down my throat. It is more bitter than metallic. How many bullets can I swallow? I know they aren't bullets. I know, I can't swallow enough.

I'm unzipping body bags, and they're filled with bullets.

Where did I get all of this ammunition?

Spring Cleaning

Hands reach to the back of the cabinet
Close on darkness
Close on shadows
The only thing that stays are shadows
How they hang against the body
How they open wide like the mouth
Like swallowing
And,
O, the swallowing!
Darken the doorway
This skeleton shape in sharpened fractures
The cabinet is just another mouth
This cabinet is starving
For affection
For calories
The only thing that stays are the calories
How they hang against the body
How the teeth clench against them
These calories like shadows in the mouth
How they come back to haunt
Ghosts of Dinners' Past
This cabinet is just another throat
Hands reach to the back of the throat
Push at wet
Push at flesh
The only thing that stays is the fingers
How they play in the purge
How they love the feel of an exorcism
And,
O, the fingers!
O, the calories!

Insomnia meet Anxiety, Anxiety— Insomnia

I sleep like a house on fire.
What I mean is,
I sleep not at all.
I sleep like the ease of turning away from a double-fatalities car
crash.
There's blood on the carpet.
Definitely won't come out.
Windshield shivered itself into bits.
And the rafters keep crumbling.
Crumble, crumble, charred mistakes.
Too much heat to still the bones.
Too much smoke to inhale, exhale, repeat, repeat.
Eyes wide.
Like earthquake tumbles.
Seismic pulse.
Like a storm, not passing.
Like brain-thoughts, tumble-cycle spin, turn-over, spin.
Like end over end.
Eyes wide.
Mattress made of food poisoning to stomach-lining me.
I sleep like it's vomiting me up.
Or I sleep like I'm vomiting my sleep.
Or I sleep like I'm vomiting myself.
What I mean to say is
I sleep not at all.

ECHO *(echo)*

how many years do you get to hold me/
against the floor of your bedroom?

/my bones were
not built for this/
i keep thinking i can ascend to heaven and when they move the
boulder from the tomb, you'll have descended to hell, and this
will be my resurrection.
deliver us from thought/deliver us from reality.
but i still wake up three days later with the same wounds that i
fell asleep with. this is not stigmata.
ECHO - you
how long will i wake up with my knees bruised from the fall?

ECHO – didn't
and no, not that fall. there were no wings.
i've never been angelic.

ECHO - ask
but 3 feet from the bed to the floor leaves its own damage, and i
can't seem to heal.
i keep trying to drown myself in the bath. force these small
deaths from my chest. swallow something clean because
everything inside has your fingerprints. i keep trying to brush
away the spots where you linger, but there's bruising here. there's
bruising here, and i'm willing to bet you didn't realize how much
you can fit inside of a bruise. i'm betting you don't know what
hangs around under the skin after you leave. there's pent-up
aggression here.
we can dissect this/this is what nephrotic looks like.
scalpel, please?

ECHO – you

didn't ask

if you cut here, you'll see where your hands catch between
my thighs. your fingers will come across a drought, but you're
hungry, not thirsty, and you were raised to swallow a meal
without a drink. slice deeper for the moment when i realize, no
won't mean no this time. words drip around us, viscous, tangible.
remove that tissue on the right. there's an open window pouring
snow. and i always thought the white light was a myth, but i must
admit that i am blinded. there's new year's day dangling in the
air and new year's eve still clinging to your breath. and there's
bleeding now, but we can staunch that. there's screaming, but
distress is easily muted. arms, meet blanket. lungs, meet hand at
throat. mouth, meet floor. back, meet knees.

there's too much movement, and none of it is mine. i'm on my
face. i'm kissing the hardwoods, shaded crimson and oak. i am
the way my bones dig into the ground. i am the way my wrists
will stain indigo and violet for days. i am the vomit that comes
after. i am the sweat you kiss from my forehead. i am the fever
post-ascension. was that as holy for you as it was for me?

and i don't have to explain the ECHO at this point.

i didn't ask for this. (echo)

i am shirt pulled up around my wrists, twisted in stronger hand.
i am face wet, silent.

i am no/no/no/no/no please, not today. and i am the negative
until it's a double, and did i negate this somehow? and maybe
two wrongs make a right? but this isn't adding up.

i didn't ask for this. (echo)

but this is no resurrection.

I didn't ask for this. (echo)

hark, the darkness sings.

I Control

I wonder if each lash had been tainted with fiery heat. What would I be if every hand pressed too heavy against the small of my back had stayed? Left me red and shaped from scars. Each fist filled with hot coal. Every word ripping through me, a tongue of flame. I'm thinking of my body and how I'm not sure whether the outside or in would fare worse.

I'm thinking of myself as raw meat. As third-degree burns. I'm imagining there's not much skin. Shiny, pink puckers and scorched remains. I'm dreaming up new ways to replay the same marks. I am a restless search and rescue party for new ways to control the bleeding in a scientific setting. It's no secret that I'm slowly covering myself up. It's no secret that I'm disappearing. But I wonder if it's still a secret that if I squint my eyes and the lighting is just right, then I swear I can see all the spots where I've been branded.

It's not quite cattle, but more of a holocaust. Permanent hemorrhages from all the times I let the injuries internalize. The bones never healed right, I know it. Brain must be liquid. Heart must be liquid. In fact, organs must be liquid. All bile and blood, with no muscle or tissue.

I know it started when I was small, but when did I start? When did I become my own abuser? Does theory and hypothesis count as control? If I incite the riot, does the push still count as shove? If I say "choke me" does it count as an experiment rather than target practice? If I batter my body and I search out the thrashings, when do I become the perfect shape?

Please Take Your Ghost from My Son

It's October, and I'm thinking about how you haven't seen your
son in five years. I'm thinking of how his eyes and his mouth are
both the shape of mine, but how the way he holds them
is nothing like the way I hold my own. I'm thinking of heavy
shadows behind his 9-year-old eyes. Of the freckles that dust his
nose that clearly does not belong to me. I'm traveling backward.
And it's October. And I'm thinking of your hand on my swollen
belly. I'm thinking of how I wasn't ready. I wasn't ready. I wasn't
ready. And, I wasn't ready. But there's your hand over my mouth,
so the words sound muffled. Your hand on the back of my neck.
Your hand too strong. And how I always blame everyone and
everything but you. It wasn't your fault. It was Corporal Hayden's
fault for getting shot in front of you and not being able to stop
himself from bleeding out. It was your mom's fault for being
raped in front of you. It was the alcohol's fault. Or it was my
fault. It was the truck you totaled. It was the way my wedding
band always sat too loose and how it was so easy to throw back at
you. It was Jeffrey's fault for waking you up screaming all of those
nights. Or maybe it was your dad's fault for making you think
that strong hands counted for something more than skin and
bones and tears. It's October, and I'm thinking of how my body
felt betrayed as it expanded to fit the shape of something that I
never asked for. It's October, and I'm thinking of how that shape
has your hairline and something behind his eyes. It's October,
and I'm finally blaming you for all the things that you stole.

12 Out Of 13

test results are not an indication of mental disorder
please seek professional advice
HIGH RISK
my mouth is dry
why is my mouth so fucking dry?
there were other tests
take another test
question one
yes
yes
yes, yes, yes,
i don't know, is that a yes?
maybe just put no, you can always change it later
do you feel like yourself?
do you know the way blood sounds in your ears?
at night, do you find that you cough out fire?
does your skin drip heat?
lay there wet and freezing while your insides scream at your
blood to burn?
do things crawl under your ribs?
but is it snakes or is it bugs?
and does it depend on what part of the body?
was someone talking? i think someone was talking, and they
must have been talking, are you writing, again? listen, i'm talking
and listen, listen, you have no fucking idea what it is to have
so many fucking bees in your head, and you keep trying to let
them out, but some asshole keeps fucking dripping honey into
the exit of the hive so they clot up like amber-fossil-sap, and it's
official my mind is crystallizing sugar again, and it's all honey-

comb solidified on the outside but inside is whirlpool-boiling,
stop fucking talking why are you always talking? and someone is
definitely talking
and question eleven
yes
yes
yes
HIGH RISK
seek professional advice
and i'm having a funeral
coffin-closed
myself as myself
but who will give the eulogy?
there are so many fucking candles here
who brought the candles?
where did all this fire come from?
i never agreed to a vigil

They Shut Off the Electric, Again

Pop. Pop. Dry swallow. And I've heard there's more than this.
But I was breaking before I knew what it was. I was born on the
wrong side of an empty milk carton. I was born as a silent Amber
Alert. Eyes too vacant to exist. Missing person: don't call, if
found. Dial-tone: disconnect. Because, hey, it's not like the phone
bill got paid, anyway. I learned how to walk in 400 square feet of
rent was late. My first words were a lie. I knew that the bathtub
is where you hide during a storm. And not just tornadoes and
earthquakes. Porcelain coffins are security
blankets during screaming matches too. And blood is red. I don't
care who told you it was blue. White walls look better in red. I
don't fucking care who said blue. The only blue I know are the
lights that spin on car-tops when there's too much broken glass,
and you can't pry guns from shaking fingers. My hands knew
how to construct stars before I could write my name. They come
from explosion. Not combustion. They come from fists through
walls and how you can hide from them if you press palm to eye
socket the way you dig your heels into the earth when it's time
to go home. Palms to eyes. And that's how stars learn to dance.
That's a waltz I learned by heart, long before I ever knew music.
And sometimes that party can show up unexpectedly. Like when
the pressure around your throat leaves less than enough space
for oxygen molecules. Those stars often burst across cheekbones.
Pour out eyes to rest as capillary-constellation against high
arches and around suitcase-laden lashes. Which while we're
on the subject, is one of many excellent spots to carry baggage.
Why sleep when the windows to my soul love to rest on a velvet
backdrop of shadow-drenched pillows? Another place with a
deep luggage wrack is the neck. And my spine is a storage unit of

depression-shaped, cardboard boxes. Most are water-logged, as oftentimes the pipes back up, and saltwater has very few places to hide in a body that is mostly skin and bone. But never mind all of that. I know a head-spin, downward spiral just as well as the next plane crash. And with no parachute, you can only go south from here. Islands are for the lonely, and I've slept on beaches with the hope of saving the sand to freeze my hourglass. But that mostly ends in breaking. Because mostly I end in breaking. I've slept in dustbin-arms after brooms I never asked for swept me into hasty, dirt piles. And sometimes those lines that rest at the edges but never quite make it in, have ground themselves across the floor with such force that the remains are like razor-cut snow. And when I press my fragmented pieces against the mirror, I know what it feels like to pass through the nasal passage as a powdered mood enhancer. I know how to feed an addiction better than I've ever fed myself. I am the number of calories I burn in direct correlation to the amount that passes down my throat. Nothing fucking else. So when you tell me that you need me, I imagine you must be starving. But there is not much of me here to feast upon. I was grown from dirt floors. My roots are deep. But I was birthed from the seed of broken home. My petals were lack-of-water, decaying before my blossoms fully bloomed. My vines have only ever pumped poison. And they have splayed themselves as ground-coverage because I beg to be walked upon. Sun, no longer touches my edges because the tree coverage grew in dense with the way I have been filled with the things I never wanted. And weeds don't leave. They spread. They tangle. But they are weeds, nonetheless. And I will only die by fire. Scorched-earth. Smoke-filled. And it all lays heavy. My body is transmission-failure immobile. Anchor-down, stationary. Respite is a peppermint spotted sun, bite-size and quick to slip down my throat. There is not burning as it scrapes the walls, but it is after-taste bitter at the back of my mouth. And it is everything I will never eat and all the guilt that I have already swallowed. And tell me again about how there's more than this. Remind me. There's more than this.

A Letter to My Suicidal Thoughts

It's not a cry for help as much as it is a birthing of blood and death. It's less of an eviction notice and more of a scene at the dinner table. It's me saying, I don't have room for you, please leave. It's a closed-door session with me as the therapist to depression and anxiety, and I'm really not sure how open they'll be with you in the room. Grief counseling started on April 27th, 2018 in the room next door, and I think you should try your luck there. I heard they have better refreshments anyway. Sometimes, when I put my ear against the wall, I still hear the heart monitors stop their incessant beeps for long enough to scream. There's way more activity there. I can't even get coffee made in this room.

Volcanology

i keep trying to triage these injuries, but i can't seem to place them in order of urgency. i linger over old damage like we never left the emergency room. like we're still barely twenty, wrapped around each other's fingers. until we're too afraid to touch

/until skin is a holy thing/until skin is a sacred thing/

until we're sewing ourselves together in sloppy stitches, pulling the thread taut. Sutures, bunching, and gathering, cinching and pulling

/until our skin is all holy/until our skin is all sacred/

until i just want my skin back. and i'm ripping and itching and tearing. leaving pieces of me behind, collecting little bits of you to cling to later. and it's a rough edge, so it'll never heal properly. i'm rebuilding, but it's too pink, shiny, new. too smooth, too tight, too raw. it's skin begging to break. but the scars built themselves into the connective tissue, and the grief goes down deep. so instead of splitting, it's constant pressure, poised to erupt. and the fault line holds with the magmatic intrusion of leftover-you. so this is years of holding me together when i just want you to let go. when i just want to fall apart

/until my skin is a holy thing/until my skin is a sacred thing/

until i'm begging for a tectonic shift. and i know, that's not how this works, but it's a common belief that a volcano remains active for ten thousand years, and even more common is that the classification of dormancy is meaningless, as a disturbance can occur at any time

/and i can't help but wonder if my memory and your ghost become a holy thing/if my memory and your ghost are a sacred thing/

if my memory and your ghost converge, does it still make a sound?

For Emily When She Is A Little Older

I am a fucking coward. I'm boarding the plane. And I'm crying.
And I'm boarding. And we're flying. But I never get off. Never
unfasten seatbelt. Did I ever fasten it, to begin with? I don't plan
on landing. This flight is headed straight to the hospital, and if
the tail-spins and turbulence are any indications, we are coming
up quick on the past, and I just don't think I'm ready for time
travel. I'm silencing my phone, but I never switch off airplane
mode, so it's irrelevant. I'm living between destinations. I'm
living between sick-bed visits and pill bottles. I'm avoiding the
way the heart monitors all make the same sound as the lights and
alarms, telling me to put my oxygen mask on first. Mine never
even drops. I'm crying. And I never exit to Terminal C. But I'm
in the cab, now. So it looks like the past caught up anyway. And
I'm crying. But I will not leave this car. I know what that waiting
room looks like. I know it is dense air. Sticky seats. I know there
is not enough coffee in the machine on the right. I know I can't
drink the coffee. The airbag light is on when I slam my head
into the dash. And I am not leaving this car. But the airbag light
was on. So, I spin out the windshield. Limbs, shaking. Hairline-
fractured as far as the eye can see. I'm bleeding in the street.
That's $30, is right here, ok? Please, don't make me leave this
car. My feet are echoing down the empty hall. I'm flooding the
elevator. I'm collapsing against the hospital bed. I'm screaming.
I'm begging. I'm not crying. I'm choking. I'm vomiting. I'm
somewhere else. I'm flying. I'm falling. I'm spinning. I'm
breaking. I'm breaking. And I swear that's broken glass, not tears.

Radiate

It's winter, but I'm breathing the hot way you made me smell in
summer. Cigarettes linger on my hair. But I've never smoked
anything other than you. So really, it's a broken boy with alcohol
breath, and a bloody nose that is clinging to the strands. It's a
chemical burn that settled in my lungs, and I breathe it out and
suck it down, and it sticks. It sticks. Heat smells the way my body
throbbed and cried with a hunger for skin to skin, and I smell
like heat. The spots between my fingers, soft webs, thin-veil of
where your hands belong, smell like heat. And where my neck
and collarbones touch, fathomless dipping-pools of salt, one
thousand leagues under all the places you should still yearn to
touch me, smell like heat. You're dripping from my pores. I'm
sweating sweet beaches and the weight of charred men. I'm
sweating the way the drugs burned your skin and how your tears
and your blood always burned mine. I'm sweating the hot way
you made me smell in summer. I'm sweating heat. I'm sweating
grief. I'm sweating blood. I'm sweating copper. I'm sweating
fire. I'm sweating you. I'm sweating me. I'm sweating heat. I'm
sweating heat.

Why I'll Always Be Haunted

i.
hands
too many hands, touching all the wrong spots. too much
pressure, in places that never asked to be stained with dirty
fingerprints and filthy mouths.

ii.
nights i woke up blindfolded. nights i woke up deaf. nights i
woke up screaming. nights i woke up dead. nights i never slept.

iii.
the way the refrigerator felt pressed up against my back.
anorexic-spine refusing to bend and break. chin up, tears
checked. the way that the solid object gave false confidence. the
way my bones still cracked.

iv.
the wedding ring in the grass.

v.
tubes & wires
small lungs failing. because babies don't belong here this early.
but trauma has a way of bringing out the best of us.

vi.
tubes & wires
"you can't hold him."
"please give me back my baby?"
"you have nerve damage."

"give me my baby back!"
"someone put her back to sleep."

vii.
distance and space and sirens and screams. and how all of those
words just feel like the word abandoned. and how everyone
always leaves.

viii.
all these fucking metaphors.

ix.
my wrists tied to his knuckles. and how he hangs around my
neck. and how he hangs around my thoughts. and how he gets
hung up in my throat. and how my eyes feel hung out to dry.

x.
the way the mirror explodes when it sees my face. how two of my
fingers fit so perfectly at the back of my mouth. how i reach for
the devil and up comes the ache.

Cleaning House In A Broken Home

I don't need two bedrooms. The first is quite cosy and bright. I'd like to get rid of the darker one. It's unnecessary.

Ma'am, that's not how this works.

Well, two bedrooms is not working for me. This second one is just sucking up all of my energy.

Ma'am, I think somewhere some information was misconstrued. We just supply your fuel.

Right. I don't want to fuel this room any more. I don't need an extra room.

Maybe you should try calling your landlord? It sounds like you need a smaller property? Unfortunately, we can't help if you have too much space to manage.

I don't rent. I bought this space. The bank said I can't just return it. I'm hoping you can just stop fuelling the extra space. I just want it to go away.

Miss, I have no way to only provide fuel to some areas. Could you just avoid that room?

I've tried that. It's just that it keeps sucking up the rest of my house.

You've lost me.

At night. I spend all day cleaning and tidying. Especially in this extra room. I empty it out. I throw out things I don't need. I lay down in bed, and I can't sleep. I get up to check the room, and it has pulled everything it finds interesting back out of the trash and the gutters. Then I have to clean it all up again before I can sleep.

Maybe you could call a realtor? Just get rid of the whole thing, and start over?

Yes. I thought that as well. This is actually my third house. I used to have a one bedroom, but it couldn't contain me. I bought a two bedroom to move some of my mess into, and it seems to be following me. I dumped it all before I bought this new home, but when I got here the second bedroom was already filling up. I'd like to cut off all power to this room. It should be vacant. Then I might sleep.

Ma'am...

Never-mind. I'll just move some things around, turn off the lights, put the music up a bit louder. Maybe I will be able to drown out whatever is going on in there until morning. I'm a bit worn out.

That sounds like a great idea, miss. Good luck.

Thanks, but I'm sure I'll call back tomorrow.

Whelm

I have always weighed myself. Sometimes in pain and ache.
Occasionally in an inundating lust for loss. But most often in
disgust. Today I saw the scales tip in favour of a tidy 30 pounds
of abhorrence. And I think of how just 30 pounds back I still
weighed at least 10 too many. And before that it may have been 5
and occasionally 10, but it has never been a thin, slim zero. The
integers have never been positive in my favour. I am negative
in self-worth. I am fractions, overwhelmed. 5s over 3s. I am the
space that I fill, and it has always been too much, though I am
still somehow never quite enough. And I sometimes wonder if
that is because I have left my more worthy pieces drowning in
porcelain pools and occasionally scattered across untouched
plates. I have clawed to the back of my throat searching for the
gods that might dwell there, and I have always come up short,
retching out demons and hail and plagues. My mouth pours only
self-taught lies and acid-suicides. And my stomach often growls.
Discontent turning of aching hellhounds, attention-starved. And
I am scratching the sky for wishing-stars, wanting for hands that
might be large enough to hold me so that when I compare them
to the mirror, I seem to disappear in contrast. But I only ever
find the hands that leave me littered in violence. The ones that
welt red and blossom indigo and violet. My skin, constellations
with velvet bruises as the always-too-heavy backdrop. More
visible than ever. My mind, raw meat. And all of me too little to
fill up anyone but myself, all overfilled, too much. Until I spew
it from my pits. And the next time my nails touch the wet cave
of my mouth, in search of reoccurring dreams, I hope that they
whisper a prayer to that devil inside. Come forth and swallow me
whole. Let me ache inside you, for once. Me as null. Me as void.

Me, disappearing. Me, disappeared. Swallow me whole. Swallow me whole.

Hands To The Sky

I crawled under the table. And that was my first mistake. Small hands and small face followed me. Knees met the carpet next to my own. Smile with missing teeth. It's that crinkled nose and squinty eye, toddler grin. And I'm whispering, no. I'm, please go back. I'm, why are you always following. I'm, OK fine, but please be quiet. I'm setting her in my lap. I'm finger to lips, shushing. And stockinged-legs are crossing and uncrossing. Crossing and recrossing.

Name of Father.

And they're noticing we're missing. And fists are banging. And voices are raised. And she's begging him to keep it down. And she's, please don't make a scene. She's, they're just babies. She's, we never go out any more. And he's fists. He's growling. He's not words. He's noises.

Name of Daughters.

And now there's no gummy smiles. There's only wet eyes. There's only tantrum. There's only kicking feet. There's four hands. Two holding the table down. Two praying. Two pleading. There's the two raising hell. There's the two ready to send the table end-over-end. There's the two that will teach something that sticks longer than what we learn in Sunday school. There's, just wait until we get home.

Name of Holy Spirit.

I catch a heel to the mouth as the table is shaken. And I never know whose heel.

Amen.

Stints

Toothpicks.
The boy leaves.
Toothpick.
You burn a body filled with poison then stick it in a jar.
Toothpick.
The girl that helps you find light is distant.
Toothpick.
The music burns your ears and your eyes.
Toothpick.
The man drinks.
Toothpick.
The queen is filled with directionless rage and tears.
Toothpick.
The boy never flies home to you.
Toothpick.
Pills and a bath just hit pause but not stop.
Toothpick.
Words. And words. And words.
Toothpick.
The sisters fight.
Toothpick.
And hospitals.
And toothpicks.
And keep boarding flights.
And toothpicks.
And you're never quite sure which hand you want to hold.
And toothpicks.
And toothpicks.

And toothpicks.
And no never means no.
And toothpicks.
And the shadows and disease and poison comes for everyone
you love.
And toothpicks.
And the hearts close up.
And toothpicks.
And toothpicks.
And toothpicks.
Toothpicks.

Seasons' Greetings

this cold is far too abundant. there's so much winter left, but i'm still mid-summer.

/i haven't even made it to fall/

my limbs are still all underneath-green. all new-birth and life.

/do you know what the shock of constant snowfall does to hot-blooded saplings/

i'm bending and breaking under the crush of frost-permeated boughs. heavy-drift, weighing down my softer parts.

/and sure, in autumn i would be just as likely to snap/

but that's a clean break. that's bones, brittle and frozen to a crystallized ache, splitting without the rough edges. summer drenched in blizzard creates tears. it is sinew and tendon-shards still clinging to one another. it pulls and stretches, all supple arches and willowy-give.

/and it's the shredding that aids the lingering/

do other people hold on the way that i do?

Hi, Dad Soup

The wires are crossed again, but the static is more of a blush.
More of a fog. Fact or fiction? Fiction or fact? Remember the
way the TV fell. That's the secret. That's the key. How it fell. How
it tumbled. How you wrote it end over end, but it was more of a
cannonball. How you dropped it from the window, but it really
was pulled from the dresser. Black-box static as the door to the
other side. Remember the clammy wet that your feet left in the
veneer top. Remember the hands over mouth. Remember the
head in the knees. Remember the balcony. Remember to look
down. Remember the face on the ledge below. Remember the
pot on the stove. Remember the clammy wet. This is what smoke
smells like. This is how you'll remember blood. This is how
you'll remember sound. This is how you'll remember bottles and
Sunday cartoons. This is where you'll remember how the colors
can all turn red. This is where you'll learn about stars behind
eyes. This is where you'll learn how the hurt gets in. How it leaks.
How you're all built from cracks. How breaking is hereditary.
And hereditary looks an awful lot like 26 letters. Hereditary
looks like all the words you can rearrange. Hereditary looks like
the whole fucking dictionary. Hereditary looks like a thesaurus
for the ways to make it mean more. It's a metaphor for the way
you're never sure if it was blood or soup. The walls are red. Is it
blood or soup?

Who Ate Who

We are midnight at the table outside. We're midnight hands-clasped. Midnight eyes-locked. Midnight bonfire-burning.

I'm fistfuls-of-pills, and you're nose-dripping-blood. And we both keep laughing. And we're smiling. And we're laughing. And we're laughing until we're crying. And we're crying. And we're confessing. And you're smoking. And you're falling. And I'm stumbling under your weight.

And I'm still Sleeping Beauty groggy, foggy, miscalculating. And you're still Snow White tittering, blithering, running in all the wrong directions. Until we're disrupt-the-party, screaming. And we're look-at-us, bodies-locked.

And it's all eyes on you. All eyes on me. It's I can't stand. And you can't sit still. And we're all eyes on each other. And we're all hands on each other. And we're all drain-circling, vomiting each other up. Fucking each other up. Fucking each other up.

Something Black & Blue

I wore bruises to my wedding.
No dress.
I wore my blood as chains around my wrists.
I wore a pregnant belly and dark circles beneath my eyes.
I wore my hopelessness like a scarlet letter.
I wore my white flag of surrender.
I wore ink on paper as a prison cell.
Or at least that's how it felt.
All I know is that there was never any dress.

Ave Maria

My mama raised me god-fearing
My mama raised me grace-filled
I will keep just the grace

Because

I drove over the quarry with nothing except death on my mind,
but god never seems to find a way to pull through, so I crossed
over instead of under, and maybe you'll say that's proof that jesus
took the wheel, but in this case I'm sure that it's not.

Because

If my body is a temple, then I am a heretic, and these are end
times for us victims of our own failures. We should be scourging
the earth. And I know all this sacrilege is supposed to sink,
supposed to crash and burn, but I never fell.

And on second thought
I will keep my mama
But who needs grace where we're headed

I drove over the quarry, but the barricade held.

Extra! Extra! Read all about it!
And it's a cry for help. But no one is dialling 911.
Bystander effect in progress.

And maybe if I give it a melody, someone will pick up the phone.
But there's no harmony in this hymn. These notes are piling.

one on top of the other, until I can't tell the difference between a symphony and the building of a mountain. They can watch from on high. I just want more viewers. My heart beat is an echo ringing through the hollow spots, a violin string snapping from excessive tension. Until, I'm not sure if my voice is cracking or breaking over the notes. Until I think I might be praying.

Until I remember, I'll only pray to my mama
Because my mama raised me god-fearing
And she's more saint-like than any grace I've ever known

So I'm begging for an exorcism.

Because no blessings could save me from this, mama.

And why didn't you perform a fucking exorcism, mama?

Because now I'm all crashing limbs and grinding teeth. Now I'm all gospel-choir call with no response. Now it's too late to pray for the sinners, mama. You pushed me down to kneel, mama. But I carry my failures on my shoulders, mama. This world is failing, mama. This weight is heavy, mama.

And now I can't stand, mama
You should have torn me at the roots, mama
Drown me still in bed, mama
Blessed are thou, mama
Blessed not is the fruit of thy womb, mama

And I'll ask you again,
Why didn't you perform an exorcism,
Mama?

Deficient

Can they diagnose me with failure to thrive this late in life? I'm in my underwear and a T-shirt again, and I'm thinking about how if the house burned down around me, it would probably leave me here. And everyone would say how it was a miracle. And I'd be expected to believe in god again. But really it'd just be my anxiety manifesting itself as the fear of being found in an emergency, looking like a total waste of breath. Really, it would just be how god always gets credit for everything I do. Like I didn't put in the fucking work. Please, devalue my time and effort. I do that to myself anyway. It was probably luck or how someone prayed for me to make it. And then, I remember how I don't have the motivation for this type of discussion, even if it's just with myself. And I think about how I wouldn't move if I smelled smoke and the room grew hot and bright with flames. Insanity is repeating the same mistake and expecting a different result, and I am a fucking riot of neurosis. Picket signs explaining why I'm not enough. But not clever ones that make you look twice. I'm like the poster board you made in the garage at 3 a.m. The kind where you wrote the letters too big to start, so now they have to cascade into scrunched-up, tiny font at the end of the line. Fuck it. I'll throw in a hyphen and hope that no one notices how all of my words are trying to get a divorce. It's not like I blame them. I'd leave me too. Too much too soon has never been enough, and I am something like a record on repeat. It's not until the needle skips that I realize exactly why I can't talk to anyone to convince them to stay. I keep saying I love you, I love you, I love you and wondering why I never seem to make it to the second verse. And then it hits me that that isn't a conversation. That's just me floundering around in the chorus. But if the room was on fire, I'd wake up right here with third-degree burns and aching lungs. I'd wake up pant-less, hopeless, useless, with my face dripping away, sloppy and slack on the left. But I'd still wake up right here. And then I think that the only reason I'd live through the house fire is because not even destruction wants to claim this mess. And how if the walls turned to smoke, I'd still find a way to drown.

Not An Official Phobia

exposure therapy (n.) if we just figure out the formula, then we can overcome this/when did this start/there is no danger/ no risk factor/similar to/autophobia, isolophobia, monophobia, eremophobia/not an official diagnosis/alone doesn't sound as bad when it is done with repetition/when did it start/can we replicate it/isolate it/no, not that type of isolate/calm down/ there's a purpose here/there has to be a purpose/how many ways are there to leave me?

i. with the fear of abandonment permanently attached to my fingertips. marry me to it. leave it caught in my throat. stain my mouth black with the word. let me hold it. make it substantial, weighty, tangible. i want to feel it sitting on my chest. let it press the life out of me. i will hold my breath and wait.

ii. when i trust you. this is challenging. this is playing the long game. this is pursuit. this is strategy. this comes after the word forever, endless, infinite. this is found at the end of gentle touches and whispered words. this is leaving during the exhale, the content-sigh. and those are rare. leave when my thoughts are clear. when the spinning has stopped. when i learn to float but before i learn to swim. when i can rely on the current but not on myself. this is leaving me with the expectation that i will drown.

iii. with ultimatums. make it my choice. i am leaving all of the leaving. this or that. that or this. they both sound like exile when you stop discriminating. add a timer for urgency. countdowns make everything sound like detonation.

iv. 3, 2, 1! do it as the new year drops in. make it a disappearing act. make enough noise, and i will never see it coming. i will still be trying to figure out the rabbit from the hat. the illusion of safety, up in smoke. i promise to search after the trick is complete. there must be a trap-door here, somewhere.

v. blindfolded. this is simple. this is exposure. this. is. exposure. hands over eyes. hands over mouth. hands around waist. hands around wrists. leave me in the dark. leave me in the tall grass. leave me in silence. dead-air, envelop me. bugs and wind and rain and heat. let the elements do the work. let the abandonment be the abandoning.

vi. as a gunshot. not me as the gunshot, but you. leave me with the explosion. leave me with the ringing. leave me with the fear of lights and sounds. this will be confusing. this will make life a balancing act with myself as the scales. the stimuli as too much or too little. is there too much or too little?

vii. before the altar. dress me in solitude, crown of thorns, stigmata hands. what was this ring for? don't board the plane. i can wait. i can wait.

viii. starving. insatiable. craving. yearning. aching. wanting. hungry. ravenous. feral. unsure.

ix. as the heart monitor sings out flatline. let me hold your hand. let me break. name yourself wind. name yourself bird-song. name yourself books and words and art. tell me we are flying. tell me it's not falling. tell me how breathing hurts. tell me it's time. tell me it's coming. tell me it's dark. leave as the heart monitor screams. alternatively known as, leave me haunted. leave me as a ghost. but is it me or is it you? it's probably both. who is haunting who?

x. in an ambulance, on a plane, in a car, walk out, crawl, run if you have to. just leave. no excuses.

xi. in pieces. leave bit by bit. first fingers, then toes. take your arms and legs. ribs are next. the veins will be problematic. i tied them into my own. excavate slowly for minimal personal trauma. cull your bones from my skeleton. they are similar at first glance, but i have carved your name in my own. look closely. take your mouth last. leave me wet. leave me shaking.

xii. with reminders wedged between couch cushions. leave your flesh in my bed. stick as smoke to my hair and my clothes. wedge your mistakes in the floorboards. brand me with disgrace. let me carry you on my skin as broken tissue. as raised and puckered. as raw and pink. i want to feel you after it starts to heal.

xiii. leave your diseases behind and buried in my veins. i will think that i have escaped. remind me that you built this.

xiv. with nightmares. wake me with clenched-fists. with bloody-throat. wake me sweating heat. again. i will think that i have escaped. remind me that you built this. remind me that you built this.

xv. more than once. i will forget the first. do it again. third time's the charm.

xvi. with all your words playing through me. let them wrap around my thoughts. i will vomit them up as my own, but we both know that they were yours. it's not a poem, more a blood-clot, and i've never known the difference. drip out of my mouth. pour out of my eyes. my nails will dig them from my skin. it's only scars here, anyway.

xvii. after sex. this is leaving with yourself as full. this is leaving with mouthfuls of honey. this is leaving after dessert. this is leaving after volcanic-end. this is leaving scorched earth. this is leaving blood. this is leaving tears. this is leaving knees bruised on hardwood. this is leaving what no longer serves you. this is leaving me breathless. but not the way i wanted.

xviii. always after sex. leave me wet. leave me shaking.

xix. when i'm least expecting it. when my back is turned. where did you go? what was this ring for?

xx. when the abandonment issues kick in. this is when i will not blame you. leave when i am already alone. leave when i only know abandoned. leave when the blindfold has sutured itself into my skin. when my hands no longer feel. leave with my ears clogged. leave with my heart beating double-time as the only song i know. leave during fight or flight. leave me when i've left myself. i won't blame you.

Use, Quit, Repeat

If I could hold your addiction, a tangible darkness, I'd drop it from shaking hands to mouth-watering tongue and swallow it whole. Let it lay heavy in my throat. Too immense to slide down my gullet. I'd take your affliction. Wide-awake, fever dreams and swollen, insomnia eyes would be easier. My insides are more stone than yours. My heart, Medusa-stare, hardened. More capable of caging that ache. Instead, I wake wet. Not sure if I am drenched in your sweat or your tears. And I fall back to sleep, uneasy. Your words laying heavy. A humid whisper that never leaves. I'm not using. And when you say it. It means you just did. I'm not using. Because I just did. And everything is numb. But it'll hurt again soon. But I'm not using. Starting tomorrow. Tomorrow. Tomorrow. Tomorrow. Tomorrow we can sleep in, because I won't wake up screaming. I won't wake up sobbing. I won't wake up shaking. Because I'm not using. I swear I'm not using. And just stay tonight. I swear I'm not using. And the sun is just a little too bright today, but I'm not using. I'm just tired. It was just a party. I'm not using. I know it was a hit-and-run, but if I stopped it'd be a whole, big thing, and I'm not using. And I didn't mean to leave you at that house, but I was in the basement, and I forgot you were waiting, and it was just one time. Tomorrow. Tomorrow. Tomorrow will be fine. And I'm sorry I stained your shirt again, but the blood will stop soon. I'm not using. And I know that you're tired, but please, just one more night. Because tomorrow is the day. And tomorrow I won't be using. I just can't sleep. And please, just sit with me. Tomorrow. I'm not using. And I'll pay you back after I turn this money around. I'm not using. And I'm just not happy. And it's not you, I swear. I love you. But could you just give me one night. Because

I'm not using. Tomorrow I'm not using. But I'm just not happy tonight. It's only because of me. It's not because of you. It's my dad and my ex and my job. And I just need to turn this money around, wait in the car. I'm not using. Just wait in the car. And I slept a few days ago. Don't worry. I'm not using. Tonight was the last time. Because I'm not using. I'm not using. I'm not using. Tomorrow. Tomorrow. Tomorrow. Gimme that tray. Hold my square.

Choke

There's bugs.

There's no bugs.

Yes, there are. There's so many that I can't breathe. They're in my chest. Under my skin. They got in through my ribs.

There are no bugs. You can breathe. You're talking to me.

…

What are you thinking?

I still can't breathe.

Yes. You're talking, remember?

Yeah, but I'm not breathing. I'm crying.

Just go to sleep. The bugs will go away.

It's too bright.

It's not. It's dark.

What if they are bugs, though? What if that's what's inside? I can't breathe. Why can't I breathe? What if there really are bugs?!

Are you there?

Wake up!

Please?! There's so many bugs…please, I can't breathe. I can't…

Over-Easy

I don't know who spilled the eggs, but I don't think "no use crying" applies here. I remember thinking I'd walk across knives. I remember thinking I'd sleep on fire. I remember thinking it was only me and you. And now I'm sticky with yolk and wishing for cleanliness. I'm feet-bleeding, taking back my promises to the sky. I'm thinking of tearing down the walls. I'm thinking of drowning in shadow. I'm thinking of abandon. I'm thinking of jumping ship. I'm thinking of rapture. I'm thinking of all of these fucking eggshells. I'm thinking of inhale. I'm thinking of exhale. I'm thinking of eggshells.

Bystander Effect

i keep starting over because these words can't find their way
i'm a disappearance, but i never meant to be

i keep starting right here because this is where i write about / it's
time to take a break / it's time to write about—

i keep running from the part where i disappear
i don't know how to write this part
it's easier to leave before impact
it's easier if i
it's easier

start over
repeat
reduce
rewind
repeat
reduce/reduce/reduce
you do not need this many lines

you only like the explosion
you're here for the finale
i know, it's hard for you to watch, but give me more lines
it's worth it if—
    never mind, here, here's the part you'll like

i wrote about how you like watching cars crash, watching trains
wreck
    because let's be honest

you're not the only one unsure of where my words were going
i don't know what that meant any better than you do
not all of these dictionaries came with maps
i'm saying that i'm not sure where i'm writing

it's like how my thoughts interrupt my thoughts before they
when i was six i / no, it's a different / that's not why you did it, it
was when / the breaks are for a reason, i just can't—

and we'll never be quite sure what i was going to say
but don't think of it as something that haunts you
think of this as a car crash
remember me as a train wreck
diffuse responsibility

someone else was probably watching

Weeds

I'm going to hit him. And he'll fucking hit me back. Because
that's what he does. He fucking hits me. But his mouth just keeps
running. And my fingers tap. And my wrists itch. And my jaw
sits tense and tight. Clenched like his fists at the end of the night.
And the truth is, I won't ever hit him. I'll come in sharp with the
words. Cut the tension of his fucking, bullshit monologue. And
as the cord snaps back, the recoil will be his hands at my throat.
And he'll squeeze too hard. Like the too-quick palm closing
over lightning bugs in summer. And he'll toss me room to room.
Dandelion seeds breaking away from the over-zealous tug. And
I'll plant blood across the threadbare, stained carpet. And they'll
bloom next spring as puckered scars across my toes. They'll
flourish, broken blood vessels below my eyes, careening across
my cheekbones. And they'll wither in the cold when the electric
in my veins is out. When there's no one home to pay the bills. As
the heat leaves me in floods. And I'll have to carry this baggage
beneath my eyes because I fear the weight of sleep. And
I'm unsure where else I can keep it. Because I've only ever owned
broken bones and tired eyes. I've only ever owned a bloodied
nose and spent muscles. So I'll gnaw at these roots that ensnare
me at the ankles. I'll rip myself from the flesh of this space. And
my mind will sleep somewhere else tonight, while my body waits
for the next gust of wind to come and plant me back across the
floor of this broken home.

And I won't ever fucking hit him.

It's a Simulation

White ladders, white mountain, white avalanche, white knight,
white nights, what fucking color is night?
It's light-sensitive. It's the way that you dull the sound. It's too
many noises thrumming in tandem. It's locked doors. It's what's
hiding behind window 357. The color of night. The color of eyes
closed. The color of weightless. It's nuclear tongue-tied ribbon, as
the unrelenting habit in the mouth of the addict. It's nagging.

It's white pills, white-hot, white-light, black-light. Glow.

My life is dripping away in watercolor spills because the acrylics
were so fucking over-enthusiastic. Charcoal stains blocking out
the sun, white-hot, charcoal stains, white-hot, spotted-suns,
white-hot.

Am I fucking art yet?

The Trigger Is In The Trauma

We're
    healing, we're healing
but the path to
    healed
is something like tumbling down the throat of a giant. Chasm of
infinity. Sempiternal-stumble. And we keep saying
    attempted suicide recovery
but the words come out choked, because if we're honest, that
noose is still neat around our necks. And how can we do
anything but stutter the words when we are so lacking in what it
takes to breathe? We keep saying
    trauma-victim survivor
like after the
    abuser
walked out the door the
    abuse
followed suit, but it's made a bed in the dark spots between our
bones. This garden is in need of culling, and we've misplaced the
means to tend these crops. And sometimes the
    suffering
is in the leaving itself.
    Abandonment
doesn't end with the closing of the book. The words pour off
the page in floods, and we don't know how to swim in oceans of
ink or how to wade through the drowning that comes from the
weight of
    alone.
We weren't built for this. We weren't built for this.

I'm Not Sorry

it's raining in the basement.
attic too.
the main floor seems...
at least something looks halfway presentable.

    if i just contain the mess/if i close the right doors

i heard a rumor, the omnipotent paid for a flood.

i did not ask for this flood.

i am prostrate in the foyer. call me inviting. call me an offering.
welcome home. it's not submission. there's nothing to see here. i
am afraid of the way that i feel too small but seem to take up too
much space all at once.

    guests track footprints across my ribs without notice / i fill
the vestibule, entirely

    you can't buy this amount of ignorance

my face is turned skyward while the ceiling falls in.

who said presentable?

the basement erupts, and i am swimming in monsoons.

    i don't know how to swim

Fretful Minds

Call it night-gardening,
But I spent my dreams planting seeds.
I tended the fields.
I culled back the weeds.
Call it selective slaughter.
Like there is not enough me for everyone else,
But,
O, how there is too much me for me!
I fill the plate,
But never sate our purges.
I swallow down.
Beg for release.
I am gnawing at the table,
Starving,
To feel anything at all.
And,
How I wish that I knew how,
To grow something worth eating.
To feel something worth growing.
To be something worth feeling!
But,
O, death-knell!
O, grave-digger!
O, monster with gnashing teeth!
What can I do, when your strength is crushing?
What can I do, when
We all think the light a thing of beauty,
Until it shines too bright?
And,

O, phoenix!
O, ash!
O, unwanted-rebirth!
What I mean is, we all want the sun to read by,
Until it burns the page into our eyes.
And,
What can I do, when
We never have enough,
Until there's too much?
O, bright and shining thing!
Am I you?
Or am I the closed-lids that shy away?
Am I the farmer?
Or the farmed?
And,
O, idle hands!
Stop planting me here!
And,
O, idle hands!
Come reap what you've sown!

From The Point Of View Of The Things I Shouldn't Think About Any More But Still Do

i.   her eyes look just like my brother's. the doorway frames her in rose, and i wonder how much she saw. is she crying or is the baby crying. her eyes look just like my brother's, and now i remember what this gun was for. i woke up to blood on the walls. i woke up screaming. i woke up blue and breathless. my brother's eyes woke to blood on the walls. my brother's eyes woke to me screaming. my brother's eyes woke to me blue and breathless. my brother's eyes can't wake. her eyes look just like my brother's. her eyes are awake.

ii.   i climb the stairs when she won't come play in the basement. it's hard to make out shadows in the dark. she'll notice me faster in the light.

iii.   she stubs her toe on the side walk. the side walks here are a mess. i hold her in my arms and carry her home, while blood drips down the block. my brother is a writer. my other brother is a mess. my sister is her best friend. my mother is a witch. her mother will push mama away. her mother will say that's dark. stop being like her. why are you like her. you remind me of her. her toe stains the bathtub. mama picks lavender from the backyard. makes her a sachet. she sleeps easy. she rarely sleeps easy now.

iv.   my eyes roll back as the neighbor boy chokes the life from me. i'm rabid. i'm scrambling. he holds my face underwater in her pool. i lay mottled. wet. i know she'll remember my eyes. she'll remember the way my fur sticks in some places, floats in others. my limbs twist into the wrong shapes. chest sunken. eyes open. she'll remember my eyes.

v.   i take the curve faster than is safe. snow sprays the night air. she loves a near-death experience. she screams with glee. why is she crying?

vi.   i tell her that never happened. she will never know what happened.

vii.   i'm drunk in the kitchen with my father's gun trained on me. i shot out the windows in her garage, but she never saw me up close. she'll dream of being the bullet in the barrel. she'll dream about my father squeezing the trigger. pops goes to jail for first degree, and the tall grass in my yard makes tall grass a trigger. tall grass is my father pulling the trigger. my brother used to skate past her house. my brother used to tell her she was sweet. tell her she was cute. the tall grass took me away. my father took us away.

viii.   her father tells her one day she'll marry me. my name tag was next to hers in class. what he should have said was one day, i'll tell her one day, but one day after many other days have passed, she will watch me through the wind shield in a parking lot as i buy my girlfriend strawberries.

ix.   i wrap my arms around her waist, hold her against the fence in her best friend's back yard. tell her i love her. tell her, one day. she cries in my shoulder. i kiss her forehead. we're too young for this. i throw her in the pool. kiss her best friend. it's not important. laugh till the day ends.

x.　　　i stole music from her locker because i missed lying next to her in bed. i never tell her that i missed lying next to her. not even when i get a second chance to lie next to her.

xi.　　　she is soft underneath me. i need her even after i marry. i try not to tell her too often.

xii.　　　i hold her down to feed her things she doesn't want. when she wakes up pregnant i perfect my disappearing act.

xiii.　　　i tell her she's dark. tell her she's wrong. tell her that's no way to live. tell her it's wrong when she doesn't want to live. she says she doesn't know how to live. i tell her she's dark. tell her she's wrong. she pretends i say the right things. she calls me vicious circle behind my back.

xiv.　　　she cries on the bathroom floor, and i don't know how to fix that, so i sleep in bed, and let her wake alone. i tell her it's her fault she's falling apart. it's her fault that i am falling apart. it's her fault that we are falling apart. most things are her fault.

xv.　　　she isn't mine, but i hold her in my car, i hold her in my bed, i hold her when she isn't around. i should keep my thoughts to myself, but i spoon-feed her sweet nothings until the sugar rush stops her heart.

xvi.　　　i bleed on her shirt. i bleed in her car. i bleed on her face and her hands and the floor and i still bleed when she sleeps.

she bleeds back into me.

xvii.   i leave on new year's eve. she tells me later how she
laid on hardwoods, stained them with oil, how her tears floated
to the surface. some spots are lighter than others. those are the
spots where i disappeared.

xviii.   i'm a double standard from across the country, but i
get around. i hang around.

xix.   we all like to hang around.
xx.   too many of us hang around.

A Guide On Saving Me

Self-care is not the same thing as self-acceptance— in which I air out the grievances I have with the miseducation surrounding mental health.

This is a poem where I drown in a sea of simplicity and am held under by "but why isn't this working for me?" The life jacket of mental health is not one size fits all, and quite a few of us have slipped through its restraints. Too often when searching for the lighthouse, I have been tempted by a whirlpool, and I have found it is full of thrashing survivors. There are some who cling to a lifeboat in the form of a bathtub and a glass of clean water, but down here at the bottom, many of us have swallowed too much salt to come up for air. The sight of your savior in the distance is only a let-down when you're unsure how to climb ashore.

And what I mean to say is, that while there is room for my person on that raft, there is no space for all of my baggage. And I tend to pack my memories in the same luggage that I store the necessities. My suitcases are filled with knots, and I am working to extract the pieces that deserve my care, but until then I am stuck failing to swim.

And what I mean is that while self-care is important, most of us will never climb up to the safety of that net until we untie our knots.

Self-care is not the same thing as self-acceptance— in which I explain why I would much rather you hand me a stitch ripper than a positive mantra.

Because this is a poem about how I need more hands to tear out years' worth of sutures. I have faced many torn edges, and I did my best to darn the holes, but I am no expert tailor. I am working at sitting with the way my fingers poke through my gloves and with the reality that sometimes my arm pushes through a hole that is not my sleeve, but I'm not quite sure that I've made peace with the reflection.

And what I mean to say is that not everyone has wounds that are easily healed, and I need you to be OK if sometimes I bleed on the carpet.

Title Me, Insignificant

I'm all recycled phrases, bullshit metaphors. Don't read me.
I'm rotting meat. Maggots in pits. I'm blood-crusted under the
surface of bruised skin. I'm broken teeth, cavities. I'm the fucking
soup du jour. But not today's. Last week's. Slop no one fucking
ate. That paper sheet on the chair at the dentist. Used. Never
changed. I'm the fever-sweat skin flakes you left in bed. Vomit
in the toilet. Bandages, bloodied. That bowl you left in your
bedroom. Covered in fucking black mold. Fucking black
mold in general. Those giant sloughs of rubber tires that litter
the freeway. Road gators. Fucking whatever. Spoiled milk.
Disposable socks at the shoe store. Those plastic sleeves that
magazines come in. Fucking useless. Empty coffee cups. Kitchen-
drawer, dead batteries. Broken light bulbs. Morning eye scum.
I'm that last sip at the bottom of the glass. No one wants to
fucking drink me. I'm last year's almanac. Last year's newspapers.
Last year's trends. Last year's date. Last year's...what the fuck was
I talking about again?

I am ruin.

Moving Under The Force Of Gravity Only

Some nights, I wake up with my hands around my own throat.
Squeeze until the insides are breaking. Windpipe, crushed.
Under-eye skin cells, bursting. Oxygen deprivation. I wait until I
feel my heart slow to a pause. Wait until my lungs ache as empty
as me. I am lack of will. My motivation clots somewhere in
between want and need and never quite flows through to raison
d'être. I don't really know how to explain to you what it's like.
It's maybe like the way that my eyes can't focus through early
morning haze. It's kind of like trying to reach something just past
your fingertips. It's like loving the ocean but only knowing how
to sink. Am I getting close? Like the way the blood feels as my
vision swims. It's like the way the air would feel underneath me
as the body rushes to concrete. Ballistic test of me. And I thought
I had this figured out. It's like how the first line rhymes with I
don't want to. And this last one rhymes with breathe.

God-Shot, Reprise

A god-shot I could eat
A god-shot to hold me
A god-shot to write
A god-shot to believe in
A god-shot with hands
A god-shot to swallow
A god-shot around the neck
Around the wrists
Down the throat
In the lungs
A god-shot to the head
To the head
To the head

About the Author

Emily Perkovich is from the Chicago-land area. She is an Art Evaluator for Persephone's Daughters and she spends her free time in the city with her family. Her work strives to erase the stigma surrounding trauma victims and their responses. Her piece This is Performance-Art was a finalist for the 50th New Millennium Writings Award and she was featured in The Divine Feminist Anthology from Get Fresh Books Publishing. She is previously published with Wide Eyes Publishing, Sunday Mornings at the River, Coffin Bell Journal, and Awakened Voices among others. Her chapbook Expulsion was released in April 2020 with Witches N Pink and her novella Swallow is forthcoming with Pegasus Publishers. You can find more of her work on her Instagram account @undermeyou.

About the Publisher

Sunday Mornings at the River is an indie poetry press founded by Rebecca Rijsdijk in 2012. It is run by poets for poets. Our aim is to create a healthy literary community in which we ourselves feel like we would be able to thrive.

We believe a poet's job is much like what Salman Rushdie wrote in his novel The Satanic Verses: a poet's work is to name the unnamable, to point at frauds, to take sides, start arguments, shape the world and stop it from going to sleep. This is the kind of poetry we are looking for and publish.

Equality and inclusivity are the magical words at our headquarters (which is an old wooden dining table with too many coffee rings on it). We believe the traditional publishing businesses hold way too much power. The only power we believe in is people power. We believe that everyone has the right to be heard, especially the people that are pushed into the shadows by the traditional publishing world. We try to amplify their voices by providing a platform and building a community, both online and offline.

We pride ourselves on being an independent publisher. We will never charge submission fees and will stay dedicated to knocking down doors and emancipating makers to publish their own poetry books without the need for a big bag of money. We are also dead serious about keeping all the rights with the makers and see ourselves as that one person we ourselves needed when we started discovering our creative nature in rural towns and far away kingdoms. None of us is in this alone.

Note on Previous Publications

"Insomnia, meet Anxiety, Anxiety- Insomnia" has previously appeared in Issue 6 of Buddy. A lit zine.

"Weeds" has previously appeared in the Domestic Violence issue of Persephone's Daughters

"They Shut Off the Electric, Again" also appeared in the Domestic Violence issue of Persephone's Daughters, as well as the anthology Prometheus Unbound

"Self-Help" has previously appeared in The Paragon Press Journal – A Conversation About Feminism

"Where It Hurts" has previously appeared in Issue 4, Memory of Tiny Spoon

"syncope" has previously appeared in io Literary Magazine

"not an official phobia" "ECHO (echo)" & "12 out of 13" have previously appeared in Emotional Alchemy Magazine

"Whir" & "ECHO (echo)" have previously appeared in the 2021 Spring Anthology of Sunday Mornings at the River

"This is Performance Art" was a finalist for the New Millenium Writings 50th New Millenium Award for Poetry and appeared in the subsequent anthology

The line "I heard a rumor" in "i'm not sorry" is taken from the graphic novel and Netflix original series The Umbrella Academy by Gerard Way

Made in the USA
Coppell, TX
21 September 2021